# The Elephant's Child

A classic tale by Rudyard Kipling
Adapted by Gill Munton

Series Editor: Louis Fidge

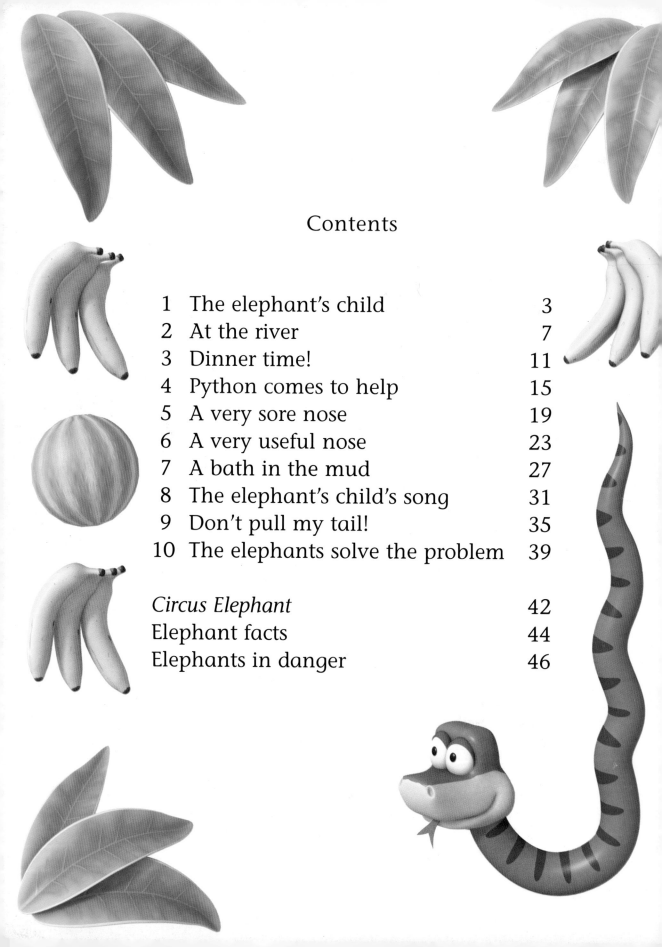

# Contents

# Chapter 1

# The elephant's child

The elephant's child lived in Africa
with Father Elephant, Mother Elephant,
and Baby Elephant.

When the world was new,
and Africa was new,
and the green, green river was new,
elephants did not have trunks.

Yes, it's true! Elephants did not have trunks!
But read the story and you will discover
how the elephant's child changed this.

The elephant's child wanted to know all about the world. He wanted to know – everything!

'Why do you have so many feathers?'
he asked his Aunt Ostrich.

'Stop asking questions, child,' said Aunt Ostrich.
'Go away! Go and see your Uncle Giraffe.'

The elephant's child went to see his Uncle Giraffe.

'Why are you so spotty?' he asked.

'Stop asking questions, child,' said Uncle Giraffe.
'Go away! Go and see your Aunt Hippopotamus.'

The elephant's child went to see
his Aunt Hippopotamus.

'Why are your eyes red?' he asked.

'Stop asking questions, child,'
said Aunt Hippopotamus.
'Go away! Go and see your Uncle Baboon.'

The elephant's child went to see
his Uncle Baboon.

'Why are melons called melons?' he asked.

Uncle Baboon looked at the elephant's child.
'Questions, questions, questions!' he said.
'Go away, elephant's child!'

One day, the elephant's child had a new question.

'What does Crocodile have for his dinner?'

'Sshh!' said Aunt Ostrich.

All the animals were afraid of Crocodile.

But the elephant's child still wanted to know.
He went to see Parrot.

'What does Crocodile have for his dinner?' he asked.

Parrot was afraid of Crocodile.
He tidied his red and blue feathers with his beak.

'If you want to know that,' he said,
'you must go to the green, green river,
and ask Crocodile.'

# Chapter 2
# At the river

The elephant's child said goodbye to Father Elephant,
and Mother Elephant, and little Baby Elephant.
He took some melons to eat on the journey,
and he started to walk to the green, green river.

It was a long journey.
As he walked,
the elephant's child ate some of the melons.

The elephant's child was always tidy,
but he left the melon skins on the ground,
because he could not pick them up.

Then he saw Python.
Python was curled up under a tree.

'Good morning, Python,' said the elephant's child.
(He was a very polite elephant's child.)
'Does Crocodile live near here?'

'What a question!' said Python.
He flicked his tail.
'What will you ask me next, elephant's child?'

'I will ask you this,' said the elephant's child.
'What does Crocodile have for his dinner?'

Python was afraid of Crocodile.

'Sshh!' he said.
Python uncurled himself very, very fast,
and slithered under a rock.

The elephant's child went on his way.
As he walked, he ate some more melons.

'No one will tell me what Crocodile has
for his dinner,' he said.

At last, the elephant's child came to the green, green river.
He saw a log of wood on the river bank,
and sat down on it.

But then the log of wood opened one eye!

The elephant's child jumped up.

'I'm sorry I sat on you,' he said politely.
'I don't know who you are, but I am looking for Crocodile.'

The log of wood opened the other eye.

'I am Crocodile!' it croaked.

# Chapter 3
# Dinner time!

Crocodile opened his mouth and laughed.
The elephant's child saw his big, sharp teeth.

The elephant's child was afraid.
But he still wanted to know what Crocodile had
for his dinner.

'Ah! **You** are Crocodile!' he said.
'Thank goodness! I have found you at last!
If it isn't too much trouble, can I ask you a question?'

'You can,' croaked Crocodile.
'What is your question, elephant's child?'

The elephant's child said, 'My question is this.
Wh-what do you have for your dinner?'

Crocodile laughed again.

'Come closer, little one,' he croaked.
'I can't hear you.'

The elephant's child went closer.
He asked his question again.

'Come closer still, little one,' croaked Crocodile.
'I can't hear you.'

The elephant's child went closer still.
He put his head right next to Crocodile's mouth.

He asked his question again.

'What do you have for your dinner, Crocodile?'

Crocodile opened his mouth.
He laughed and laughed.

'I will tell you what I am going to have
for my dinner today!' he croaked.
'I am going to have – an elephant's child!'

And then he grabbed the elephant's child's nose
between his big teeth – snap!

'Let go! Let go!' squeaked the elephant's child.

But Crocodile just laughed.

# Chapter 4
# Python comes to help

Python heard the noise,
and slithered out from under his rock.
He slithered to the green, green river.

He was afraid of Crocodile,
but he wanted to help the elephant's child.

'Pull, elephant's child!' he said.
'Pull as hard as you can!
If you don't, Crocodile will eat you!'

The elephant's child pulled one way.
Crocodile pulled the other way.

The elephant's child pulled harder.
So did Crocodile.

As they pulled, the elephant's child's nose
s-t-r-e-t-c-h-e-d into a long trunk!

But then his feet started to slip in the thick, brown mud.

'Help!' he squeaked.

Python slithered down the bank.
He curled round the elephant's child's legs.

The elephant's child pulled.
Python pulled.
But Crocodile pulled harder.

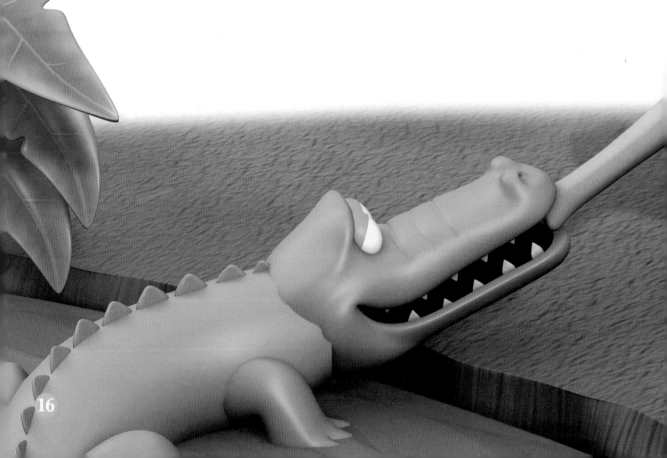

Parrot heard the noise.
He was afraid of Crocodile,
but he wanted to help the elephant's child, too.
He flew over the trees to the green, green river.

Parrot grabbed Python's tail in his beak.

The elephant's child pulled.
Python pulled.
Parrot pulled.
But Crocodile pulled harder.

Aunt Hippopotamus was swimming
in the green, green river.
She heard the noise.

She ran along the river bank.
She slid down the river bank.
She grabbed Parrot's tail in her mouth.

The elephant's child pulled.
Python pulled.
Parrot pulled.
Aunt Hippopotamus pulled.

And this time, Crocodile opened his mouth and let go.

The elephant's child,
and Python,
and Parrot,
and Aunt Hippopotamus
all fell back into the thick, brown mud.

Plop! Plop! Plop! **Plop**!

# Chapter 5

# A very sore nose

'Thank you, my friends,' said the elephant's child.
'Crocodile can't eat me now.
But look at my nose!'

They all looked.

'It's – very long,' said Python.
'It's as long as my tail!'

'It's – very red,' said Parrot.
'It's as red as my feathers.'

'It's very sore,' said Aunt Hippopotamus.
'I will wrap it in banana leaves.
That will make it better.'

So Aunt Hippopotamus wrapped
the elephant's child's nose in banana leaves.

'Now dip your nose in the river,' she said.
'That will make it feel cool.'

So the elephant's child dipped his nose
in the green, green river.

He sat there all day.

'My nose is not so sore now,' he said.
'And it feels nice and cool.
But it's still very long!'

He sat there all night.

'My nose is not sore at all now,' he said.
'But it's **still** very long.
It looks ugly!
And it will get in my way.
When will it be short again, Aunt Hippopotamus?'

'I don't think it **will** be short again,'
said Aunt Hippopotamus.
'You will always have a long nose, elephant's child.
Go home now, and be happy with your new, long nose.'

So the elephant's child plodded up the bank
of the green, green river, and set off for home.

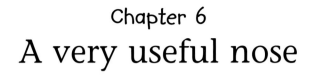

# Chapter 6
# A very useful nose

It was a hot morning.
And it was a long journey home.
The elephant's child plodded along
under the banana trees.
He wished he was home with the other animals.

Lots of flies flew round the elephant's child's head,
or sat on his back.
He flicked them away
with his long trunk.

'That's better!' he said.

Soon it was afternoon.
The elephant's child was hungry.

'What can I have for my dinner?'
he said. 'I have eaten all the melons,
and I still have a long journey.'

Then he saw some nice green grass.

He stretched out his long trunk
and picked some grass.

He put the grass in his mouth,
and started to eat.

'Mmm!' he said. 'That's better!'

The elephant's child went on his way.

Suddenly he stopped,
and looked down at his long, grey trunk.
He curled it this way and that.

'Maybe my long nose can be useful after all,' he thought.
'I can flick away flies with it,
and I can pick grass with it.'

# Chapter 7
# A bath in the mud

The day got hotter and hotter,
and the elephant's child plodded on.

He came to a muddy green pond.

He dipped his long trunk into the cool, green pond.
He sucked up some mud,
and squirted it all over his head and his back.
The elephant's child had a bath in the mud!

'That's better!' he said.

Soon it was evening.
The elephant's child was hungry again.

'What can I have to eat?' he said.
'I have eaten all the grass,
and I still have a long journey.'
Then he saw some yellow bananas in a tree.

He stretched his long trunk up into the tree
and picked the bananas.

He put them in his mouth, and started to eat.

'Mmm!' he said. 'That's better!'

The elephant's child went on his way.

Suddenly he stopped,
and looked down at his long, grey trunk.
He curled it this way and that.

'Maybe my long nose is not a bad thing after all,'
he thought.
'I can flick flies away with it,
and I can pick grass with it,
and I can squirt mud with it –
and I can pick bananas with it!'

# Chapter 8

# The elephant's child's song

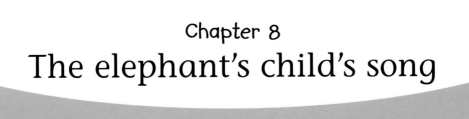

Soon the elephant's child came to a little stream.

'I have eaten lots of green grass,
and lots of yellow bananas,' he said,
'and now I am thirsty.'

He stretched out his long trunk
and dipped it into the cool stream.
He sucked up some water
and squirted it into his mouth.

'Mmm!' he said. 'That's better!'

'I'm nearly home!'
the elephant's child said happily.

He was so happy that he started to sing!

'La la, la la, la la!
The elephant's child is walking along.
He's singing a happy elephant song ...'

But his voice sounded strange.
It sounded – loud. Very loud.

'It must be my new nose!'
said the elephant's child.
'It makes my voice very loud –
like a trumpet!'

He looked down at his long grey trunk.
He curled it this way and that.

'Maybe a long nose is –
the best nose to have!' said the elephant's child.
'I can flick flies away with it,
and I can pick grass with it,
and I can squirt mud with it,
and I can pick bananas with it,
and I can squirt water with it,
and I can sing with it!'

He trumpeted and trumpeted.

And then he saw some melon skins on the ground.

He picked them up with his long grey trunk.
(He was a very tidy elephant's child.)

# Chapter 9
# Don't pull my tail!

When he arrived home,
the elephant's child trumpeted loudly.

The other elephants ran to see him.
They wanted to hear his story.

'Did you go to the green, green river?'
asked Father Elephant.

'Yes, I did,' replied the elephant's child.

'Did you see Crocodile?' asked Mother Elephant.

'Yes, I did,' replied the elephant's child.

'Why is your nose so long?'
squeaked little Baby Elephant.

'When I asked Crocodile what he had
for his dinner, he grabbed my nose.
He pulled and pulled it.
He stretched my nose and made it longer,'
said the elephant's child.

'It's very ugly,' said Father Elephant.

'Yes, it is,' said the elephant's child.
'But it's very useful.
I will show you what I can do.'

He grabbed Father Elephant's tail
with his trunk.

'Ouch!' said Father Elephant.
'Don't pull my tail!'

Then the elephant's child turned to Mother Elephant.
He stretched out his trunk and poked her.

'Ouch!' said Mother Elephant.
'Stop it! Don't poke me again!'

The elephant's child laughed,
and wrapped his trunk round Baby Elephant.
He picked him up, and threw him into a bush.

'Ouch!' squeaked Baby Elephant.
'Stop it! Don't do that again!'

But the elephant's child did not stop.
Every day, he made trouble with his new nose.
He grabbed, and he pulled, and he poked, and he threw.
And all the time, he trumpeted.
Very loudly.

'What can we do?' asked Father Elephant.
'We must make him stop!'

'It's his new nose!' squeaked little Baby Elephant.
'His new nose is making him bad.'

'Yes,' said Mother Elephant slowly.
'And I know what we can do ...'

# Chapter 10
# The elephants solve the problem

Next morning, the three elephants set off.
Father Elephant went first, then Mother Elephant,
then Baby Elephant.

It was a long way.
But at last, they came to the green, green river.
Crocodile lay in the mud, fast asleep.

He opened one eye.
'Elephants!'

'Good morning, Crocodile,' said Father Elephant.
'We think we can help you –
if you will help us.'

'I don't like elephants!' said Crocodile.
'Well, I like them for my dinner –
but that's all.'

'What other things do you like to eat, Crocodile?'
said Mother Elephant.

'Well – I **do** like bánanas …' said Crocodile, slowly.

'If you stretch our noses,' said Father Elephant,
'we will reach up into the trees
and pick some bananas for you.
You can have bananas for your dinner every day!'

And so Crocodile grabbed the nose of each elephant,
and pulled, and pulled, until it was a long trunk.

So all the elephants had long trunks.
When they got home, they all lived together peacefully.
There was no more grabbing, or pulling,
or poking, or throwing.

And that is the story of how the elephant got his trunk.

**Elephants use their trunks every day –
for flicking flies away,
for picking grass,
for dipping,
for sucking,
and for squirting.**

**And for trumpeting.**

**And for …
picking bananas!**

# Circus Elephant

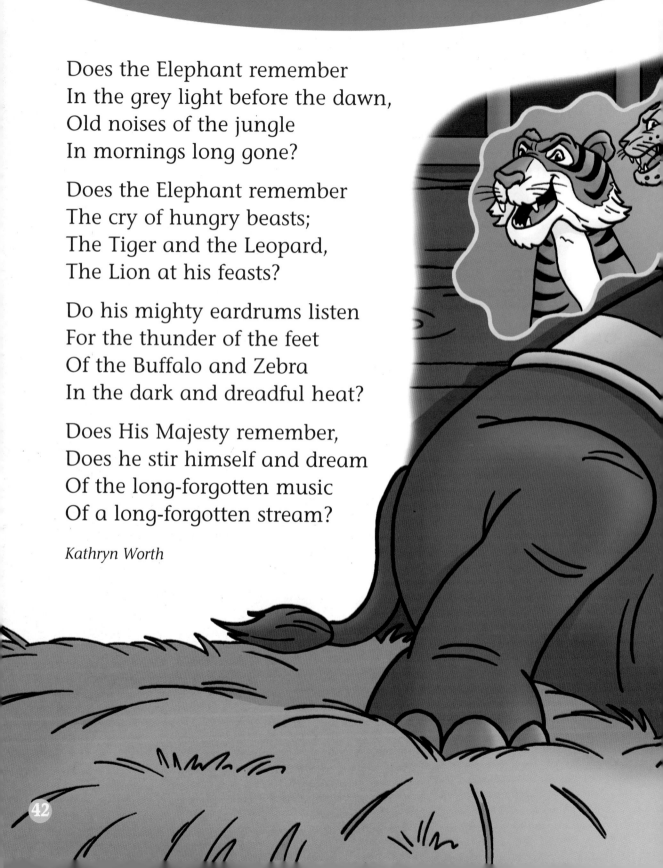

Does the Elephant remember
In the grey light before the dawn,
Old noises of the jungle
In mornings long gone?

Does the Elephant remember
The cry of hungry beasts;
The Tiger and the Leopard,
The Lion at his feasts?

Do his mighty eardrums listen
For the thunder of the feet
Of the Buffalo and Zebra
In the dark and dreadful heat?

Does His Majesty remember,
Does he stir himself and dream
Of the long-forgotten music
Of a long-forgotten stream?

*Kathryn Worth*

# Elephant facts

The elephant is the biggest land animal in the world.
A big African elephant weighs 7,000 kg.

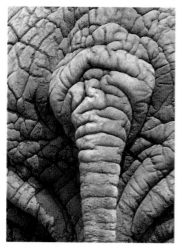

An elephant's skin is 3 cm thick.

An elephant can run 40 kilometres an hour.

An elephant's tusks never stop growing.

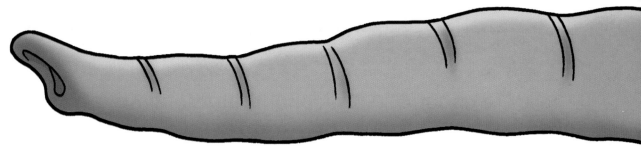

## Trunk facts

An elephant's trunk is made of muscle,
and it is really the elephant's nose and top lip.

The elephant uses its trunk for:

- picking plants and taking them to its mouth

- having a mud bath or a dust bath

- taking water to its mouth

- trumpeting

An elephant's trunk can pull up a tree –
or it can pick up a pin.

When an elephant lifts its trunk into the air,
it can smell food, or danger, from a long way away.

# Elephants in danger

There are about 40,000 elephants in Asia and about 500,000 elephants in Africa.

People are building more and more towns and roads, and the elephants are slowly losing their homes.

Some elephants eat food from farms when they are hungry. Some farmers shoot the elephants.

Some people hunt elephants because they can sell their tusks.

If an elephant mother is injured or killed, her baby is in danger.

# An elephant sanctuary

These elephants live at an elephant sanctuary.
At the sanctuary, the elephants are safe.
No one can hunt them or shoot them here.

Every year, about 50 elephants come to live here.

Some of them are very old, some are injured or sick,
and some are babies.

Each adult elephant in the sanctuary needs 200 kg of food
and 190 litres of water every day!

The baby elephants drink milk from giant bottles.

Every day, the elephants have a cool bath in the river.

Macmillan Education
Between Towns Road, Oxford OX4 3PP
A division of Macmillan Publishers Limited
Companies and representatives throughout the world

ISBN 978-1-4050-6009-7

First published 2006

Design and layout by Anthony Godber
Illustrated by Jonatronix Ltd and Simon Rumble
Cover design by Linda Reed & Associates
Cover illustration by Jonatronix Ltd

The authors and publishers would like to thank the following for permission to reproduce their
photographic material:
Alamy pp44(t), 46(br), Corbis pp44(bm, br), 46(tr, tl, bl), Photolibrary.com pp44(bl), 47

The Series Editor and the Author would like to give
special thanks to Gill McLean for her contribution
in setting up the Macmillan Explorers series, for her
continuous encouragement, and for her positive and
practical help and advice throughout its production.

We are grateful for permission to reprint the following
copyright material:
'Circus Elephant' first published in *They Loved to Laugh*
by Kathryn Worth (Doubleday, Doran & Co, 1942),
copyright © Kathryn Worth Curry 1942, reprinted by
permission of Random House Children's Books,
a division of Random House, Inc.

Printed by Zamzam Presses, Egypt

2010  2009  2008  2007
10  9  8  7  6  5  4  3  2